BEFORE THE
WEDDING

FUN AND PROVOCATIVE QUESTIONS
TO PREPARE YOU FOR MARRIED LIFE

*Relive your answers
for years to come!*

By Alex A. Lluch
Relationship expert and author of over 3 million books sold!

WS Publishing Group
San Diego, California

BEFORE THE WEDDING

FUN AND PROVOCATIVE QUESTIONS
TO PREPARE YOU FOR MARRIED LIFE

By Alex A. Lluch

Published by WS Publishing Group
San Diego, California 92119
Copyright © 2009 by WS Publishing Group

Designed by WS Publishing Group:
Sarah Jang & David Defenbaugh

For Inquiries:
Log on to www.WSPublishingGroup.com
E-mail info@WSPublishingGroup.com

ISBN-13: 978-1-934386-36-1

Printed in China

CONTENTS

INTRODUCTION

You are about to embark on marriage, one of the most fantastic and exciting adventures of your lives. Perhaps you knew from the first glance that you would end up together. Or, perhaps it has taken years of cultivating trust, friendship, and love to come to this point. Whatever your course, life has led you here, together.

The trials of marriage are probably no secret to you. By now, you know that your relationship will have ups and downs, winters and summers, and you will have to weather them both, as a pair. Your marriage will know both joy and hardship, but discussing important topics now, before the wedding, will help prepare you for any situation.

As writer Leo Tolstoy, author of *War and Peace*, once said, "What counts in making a happy marriage is not so much how compatible you are, but how you deal with incompatibility." In other words, don't make the assumption that you and your spouse feel the same way about the big issues, even though you are very much in love.

It is crucial to your future happiness that you address some important issues now, even though you may be hesitant or afraid to discuss them. This book simplifies this process and even makes it enjoyable. It contains more than 400 thought-provoking, inspiring, and sometimes difficult questions that will build trust, open the lines of communication, and help solidify your bond. For instance, are you on the same page when it comes to things like in-laws, finances, and raising a family? Do you both envision the same future, 5, 10, or even 50 years down the road? What are the areas in which you and your spouse may disagree? How can you head off conflict at the pass?

A surprising number of people know less about their spouse than they do their friends. Understanding each other's expectations and discussing your hopes and dreams as a couple will help ensure that your marriage lasts a lifetime. Additionally, the questions in this book will remind you of all the little things you love and are grateful for in your spouse-to-be.

As you discuss each of the questions in this book, record your hopes, fears, and expectations. Refer back to your responses as often as you like; use them to gauge how your marriage and understanding of one another is growing and changing over time. Ask these questions again and again. Talk often. Be heartfelt. Sometimes you will laugh, and sometimes you will need to be serious. Your discussions needn't always be profound; just allow these questions to help you connect, communicate, and encourage the friendship in your partnership.

Congratulations on finding the one to share your life with. As poet Robert Browning wrote, "Grow old along with me! The best is yet to be."

Warm-Up

Discussing your future requires remembering and appreciating your past. Recall your first meeting, your first kiss, and other memories from the beginning of your relationship. Could you ever have imagined you would be getting married?

A shared history is a wonderful predecessor to a successful tomorrow. It is valuable to document falling in love, the proposal, your wedding day, and all the happy memories that will follow. Create journals, photo albums, scrapbooks, and home videos. Remember and relive all you have witnessed, created, and survived. Cherishing your past will help you look forward to what is still to come.

Of course, you have countless reasons why you love being together and make a great team and, thus, know you will make a resilient, lifelong pair. And, naturally, you have similarities and differences. You will not always see eye to eye. However, the experiences, qualities, and characteristics that led you to fall in love create the foundation on which you will build your marriage.

Cherishing the good times of your past is an important part of having a happy marriage. Use the following questions as a warm-up for the chapters that follow.

"I love you not only for what you are,
but for what I am when I am with you."

– Elizabeth Barrett Browning

Questions to Warm Up

Why do we love being together?

Partner 1: _____

_____

Partner 2: _____

_____

Why will we make a great married couple?

Partner 1: _____

_____

Partner 2: _____

_____

How did we first meet?

Partner 1: _____

_____

Partner 2: _____

_____

What did we do on our first date?

Partner 1: _____

_____

Partner 2: _____

_____

Describe our first kiss.

Partner 1: _____

_____

Partner 2: _____

_____

How did we know we were meant to be?

Partner 1: _____

_____

Partner 2: _____

_____

Who said I love you first?

Partner 1: _____

_____

Partner 2: _____

_____

Describe our reactions to saying I love you for the first time.

Partner 1: _____

_____

Partner 2: _____

_____

Why do we make a great team?

Partner 1: _____

_____

Partner 2: _____

_____

Describe an unforgettable moment thus far.

Partner 1: _____

_____

Partner 2: _____

_____

Describe one of our favorite memories.

Partner 1: _____

_____

Partner 2: _____

_____

Describe one of our funniest memories.

Partner 1: _____

_____

Partner 2: _____

_____

Describe an awesome vacation we took.

Partner 1: _____

_____

Partner 2: _____

_____

Describe how and where the proposal happened.

Partner 1: _____

_____

Partner 2: _____

_____

Describe a time we couldn't have gotten through without each other.

Partner 1: _____

_____

Partner 2: _____

_____

What is the biggest obstacle we have had to overcome?

Partner 1: _____

_____

Partner 2: _____

_____

Who are the friends and family members who are most supportive of us?

Partner 1: _____

_____

Partner 2: _____

_____

What are three things we are excited about for our marriage?

Partner 1: _____

_____

Partner 2: _____

_____

What three songs would go on the soundtrack to our relationship?

Partner 1: _____

_____

Partner 2: _____

_____

In one sentence, describe our relationship.

Partner 1: _____

_____

Partner 2: _____

_____

HOME

Your home is the sanctuary that you create. It is the safety you build around each other and your family. It will become an expression of your love and your personalities, which are always changing and evolving with time.

Even if you live together now, your married home will be and feel different. Making a home together after marriage means agreeing to share. You will choose a neighborhood, make mortgage payments, manage chores, tackle repairs, and decide on décor together. Sound easy? It never is. The old overstuffed armchair he loves may not fit with your modern taste. Without a doubt, he will be surprised by the sheer number of bath products you own.

Disagreements over color schemes will make way for the challenge of dividing household labor. How can you make sure chores are divided in a way that is fair and works for both of you? As Dr. Joyce Brothers wisely said,

"Marriage is not just spiritual communion, it is also about taking out the trash."

This discussion of home will also help manage your expectations. It is quite likely that one or both of you have been imagining your home since you were very young. Maybe one of you envisioned a big backyard with pets running and playing. Perhaps you would love space for a home office. One of you may want a large, spacious home, while the other envisions something more quaint and cozy.

How do your dreams measure up to reality? It is important to talk about trade-offs you may have to make. If it is important to buy a four-bedroom house, for example, you may end up in a less-desirable neighborhood. Do you plan to stretch your income to make a mortgage payment, or would you rather rent until you are more financially secure? Will this home be a starter home or a long-term residence? These are all worthwhile things to discuss.

You will find that talking about home reveals many of your goals and dreams for your marriage. Do you hope to save up for a second home? A beach cottage? An RV? Home represents your emotional and financial security. By discussing your hopes and expectations for your home together, you can plan for the future with common goals.

"Where we love is home,
home that our feet may leave,
but not our hearts."

— Oliver Wendell Holmes

Questions About Our Home

What will our first home look like?

Partner 1: _____

_____

Partner 2: _____

_____

Will it be an apartment, townhouse, or custom home?

Partner 1: _____

_____

Partner 2: _____

_____

Will we rent, own, or build it ourselves?

Partner 1: _____

_____

Partner 2: _____

_____

How many bedrooms will our home have?

Partner 1: _____

_____

Partner 2: _____

_____

How will it be decorated? Modern? Vintage? Classic? All white?

Partner 1: _____

_____

Partner 2: _____

_____

What colors will we paint the walls?

Partner 1: _____

_____

Partner 2: _____

_____

Will it have wood floors or carpet?

Partner 1: _____

_____

Partner 2: _____

_____

Will it have a yard? Grass? A patio? A porch?

Partner 1: _____

_____

Partner 2: _____

_____

Will our house have a swimming pool? A spa? A waterslide?

Partner 1: _____

_____

Partner 2: _____

_____

Describe our living room.

Partner 1: _____

_____

Partner 2: _____

_____

How big will our TV be?

Partner 1: _____

_____

Partner 2: _____

_____

Describe our bedroom.

Partner 1: _____

_____

Partner 2: _____

_____

What kind and size of bed will we have?

Partner 1: _____

_____

Partner 2: _____

_____

Describe our kitchen. What appliances or features will it have?

Partner 1: _____

_____

Partner 2: _____

_____

Describe the feeling of walking into our home.

Partner 1: _____

_____

Partner 2: _____

_____

What new furniture will we buy?

Partner 1: _____

_____

Partner 2: _____

_____

What old pieces of ours will we keep?

Partner 1: _____

_____

Partner 2: _____

_____

Where will our home be? In what city and state? In what part of the city?

Partner 1: _____

_____

Partner 2: _____

_____

Describe our neighborhood.

Partner 1: _____

_____

Partner 2: _____

_____

Will we be friends with our neighbors?

Partner 1: _____

_____

Partner 2: _____

_____

Who will cook meals?

Partner 1: _____

_____

Partner 2: _____

_____

How many nights a week will we have dinner together?

Partner 1: _____

_____

Partner 2: _____

_____

Who will do the dishes? Will it depend on who cooks?

Partner 1: _____

_____

Partner 2: _____

_____

Which household chores do we each like, dislike, or really hate?

Partner 1: _____

_____

Partner 2: _____

_____

How will we divide chores?

Partner 1: _____

_____

Partner 2: _____

_____

Who will do which chores?

Partner 1: _____

_____

Partner 2: _____

_____

Will we have pets in our new home? How many? What kind?

Partner 1: _____

_____

Partner 2: _____

_____

How long will we live in this home? A year? 5 years? 10 years? Forever?

Partner 1: _____

_____

Partner 2: _____

_____

If we could pick one place to live for just a year, it would be:

Partner 1: _____

_____

Partner 2: _____

_____

If we could choose one fantasy item for our home, it would be:

Partner 1: _____

_____

Partner 2: _____

_____

CHILDREN

There is nothing more rewarding than being surrounded by the warmth of a loving family, no matter how big or small. Some couples want to have children right after the wedding. Some couples decide to wait several years and relish married life. Others may agree that they don't ever want to have children. And a few of those couples change their minds down the road.

The fact of the matter is that pregnancy and raising children can add emotional, physical, and financial strain to your marriage. If you have decided you want children, how can you be sure that you experience the joyful side and minimize stress?

The key is to talk openly about your plans for child rearing and discipline and to establish a rock-solid union before welcoming additions to your family. Because you were brought up differently, you may have very different backgrounds, traditions, cultures, and religious upbringings. You may find you have some incongruent ideas about education, discipline, and other responsibilities of parenting.

However, a couple with a strong sense of "we-ness" will be better prepared for the transition into parenthood, no matter how they differ when it comes to parenting. Keep your lines of communication open at all times, and don't worry about being perfect parents. It's OK to show your children that you make mistakes, as long as you work as a team to compromise and problem-solve.

Talking through the questions in this chapter will help you understand each other's feelings and ideas about having and raising children.

"Life is magic,
the way nature works seems to be quite magical."

– Jonas Salk

Questions About Children

Do we want to have children together?

Partner 1: _____

_____

Partner 2: _____

_____

If yes, when?

Partner 1: _____

_____

Partner 2: _____

_____

Ideally, how many children do we want? How many boys and/or girls?

Partner 1: _____

_____

Partner 2: _____

_____

Do we have names picked out?

Partner 1: _____

_____

Partner 2: _____

_____

Are there any names with special significance?

Partner 1: _____

_____

Partner 2: _____

_____

How important is having children to us?

Partner 1: _____

_____

Partner 2: _____

_____

Will we consider fertility treatments if we have a hard time conceiving?

Partner 1: _____

_____

Partner 2: _____

_____

Will we consider adoption?

Partner 1: _____

_____

Partner 2: _____

_____

If we do not want children, how certain of that decision are we?

Partner 1: _____

_____

Partner 2: _____

_____

What if one of us changes his or her mind?

Partner 1: _____

_____

Partner 2: _____

_____

What will we do if we have an unplanned pregnancy?

Partner 1: _____

_____

Partner 2: _____

_____

Will either of us eventually want to be sterilized?

Partner 1: _____

_____

Partner 2: _____

_____

What are we most looking forward to about being parents?

Partner 1: _____

_____

Partner 2: _____

_____

How will having a baby change our marriage?

Partner 1: _____

_____

Partner 2: _____

_____

Who will get up in the middle of the night when the baby cries?

Partner 1: _____

_____

Partner 2: _____

_____

Who will change diapers?

Partner 1: _____

_____

Partner 2: _____

_____

Will we turn to our parents for help with the baby?

Partner 1: _____

_____

Partner 2: _____

_____

Who will discipline our children?

Partner 1: _____

_____

Partner 2: _____

_____

Is one of us a better disciplinarian than the other?

Partner 1: _____

_____

Partner 2: _____

_____

How will we punish our kids when they misbehave?

Partner 1: _____

_____

Partner 2: _____

_____

Will we spank our kids?

Partner 1: _____

_____

Partner 2: _____

_____

Which one of us will probably spoil our kids, and how?

Partner 1: _____

_____

Partner 2: _____

_____

What rules will we give our kids? No candy? No TV before homework?

Partner 1: _____

_____

Partner 2: _____

_____

What are the most important things we will teach our children?

Partner 1: _____

_____

Partner 2: _____

_____

Will we get our children pets? What kind?

Partner 1: _____

_____

Partner 2: _____

_____

If we both work, will we send our kids to daycare? Will we hire a nanny?

Partner 1: _____

_____

Partner 2: _____

_____

Will our children go to preschool?

Partner 1: _____

_____

Partner 2: _____

_____

Will our kids go to private or public school?

Partner 1: _____

_____

Partner 2: _____

_____

How old will our kids have to be before we let them stay home alone?

Partner 1: _____

_____

Partner 2: _____

_____

Will we urge our kids to play sports or instruments?

Partner 1: _____

_____

Partner 2: _____

_____

How strongly will we urge them to follow in our footsteps?

Partner 1: _____

_____

Partner 2: _____

_____

How will we be like our parents?

Partner 1: _____

_____

Partner 2: _____

_____

What do we want to do differently than our parents?

Partner 1: _____

_____

Partner 2: _____

_____

How will we make time for our children?

Partner 1: _____

_____

Partner 2: _____

_____

How will we make time for ourselves without the kids?

Partner 1: _____

_____

Partner 2: _____

_____

What special measures will we take if we have children from other relationships?

Partner 1: _____

_____

Partner 2: _____

_____

What are our concerns about having a blended family?

Partner 1: _____

_____

Partner 2: _____

_____

A letter from us, to our future child/children:

_____

_____

_____

_____

_____

_____

_____

_____

_____

_____

_____

_____

_____

_____

_____

_____

_____

Religion & Spirituality

You've probably heard people say you should avoid talking about politics and religion at all costs; however, it is imperative that you discuss religion before marriage. A divergence in religious beliefs within a couple can alienate family members, complicate raising children, and even make planning your wedding very difficult. As this book has surely shown you already, it is enough of a struggle to get past your differences in opinion and taste, let alone differences in religious background. Thankfully, if you are in a mixed-faith relationship, you're not alone. It is estimated that 40 to 50 percent of couples are in mixed-faith marriages.

Even if you don't practice a specific religion in your household, you may want to incorporate elements of spirituality into your lives. Many people consider themselves "spiritually minded" without adopting one religion or another. Your spiritual beliefs may affect your values, expectations, and goals for your marriage and other relationships.

You will find that religion and spirituality is a difficult topic to discuss in a relationship, simply because religious traditions, rituals, and beliefs have been ingrained in us since we were young children. Religion is often one of those "non-compromise" issues — areas in which people are not willing to budge, even for a loved one.

Acknowledging your differences is the first step to preventing issues with family and within your relationship. Talk openly about your religious backgrounds, including the traditions you hope to carry into your marriage and family. Do you want to raise your children in a specific religion? Might you infuse religious elements into your wedding to appease family members who are attending? What holidays will you celebrate? These are all questions to consider before marriage and later, as you decide to start a family.

In reality, you should never stop talking about religion and spirituality. Birth, illness, loss of a loved one, and other major life decisions often impact faith and religious practice greatly. Over the years, continue the conversation sparked by the questions in this chapter and you will enjoy spiritual growth as a couple.

"The best and most beautiful things
in the world cannot be seen or even touched.
They must be felt with the heart."

— Helen Keller

Questions About Religion & Spirituality

Do we both believe God exists?

Partner 1: _____

_____

Partner 2: _____

_____

Do we share the same religion? If not, do we foresee any issues?

Partner 1: _____

_____

Partner 2: _____

_____

Will we have religious elements in our wedding?

Partner 1: _____

_____

Partner 2: _____

_____

Do we attend or belong to a church, temple, or religious group?

Partner 1: _____

_____

Partner 2: _____

_____

What religious beliefs do we agree on?

Partner 1: _____

_____

Partner 2: _____

_____

What religious beliefs do we disagree on?

Partner 1: _____

_____

Partner 2: _____

_____

Do either of us have negative feelings about any specific religion/s?

Partner 1: _____

_____

Partner 2: _____

_____

How much time each day or week will we devote to spirituality?

Partner 1: _____

_____

Partner 2: _____

_____

What traditions will we incorporate into our family?

Partner 1: _____

_____

Partner 2: _____

_____

Will we say grace or nightly prayers?

Partner 1: _____

_____

Partner 2: _____

_____

Will we raise our children in a specific religion?

Partner 1: _____

_____

Partner 2: _____

_____

What religious holidays or traditions will we observe?

Partner 1: _____

_____

Partner 2: _____

_____

Will we have religious symbols in our home?

Partner 1: _____

_____

Partner 2: _____

_____

Will any portion of our income go to a religious organization?

Partner 1: _____

_____

Partner 2: _____

_____

Do we believe in Creationism or Darwinism?

Partner 1: _____

_____

Partner 2: _____

_____

Do we believe in astrology?

Partner 1: _____

_____

Partner 2: _____

_____

If yes, do we believe that our astrological signs are compatible?

Partner 1: _____

_____

Partner 2: _____

_____

Do we believe in fate?

Partner 1: _____

_____

Partner 2: _____

_____

Do we believe in destiny?

Partner 1: _____

_____

Partner 2: _____

_____

Do we believe that there is a "plan" for us?

Partner 1: _____

_____

Partner 2: _____

_____

FAMILY

You and your spouse's relationships with your families demonstrate the value you place on companionship in many ways. Evaluating the closeness and influence of your extended families will help you build a tight-knit, healthy bond between your marriage and your in-laws.

In-laws can be a source of love and support. You will cherish them if you need help with childcare, advice, or even finances. Your extended family also offers you traditions and rituals that can give you identity as a couple and as a family.

Many times, however, in-laws are a source of marital strife. We've all heard the jokes — Mark Twain once wrote, "Adam was the luckiest man; he had no mother-in-law." Indeed, it can be a feat to get along with your in-laws, but, for better or worse, your marriage comes with a new set of permanent family members.

Don't assume you are on the same page when it comes to boundaries with in-laws. To avoid the tug-of-war between relatives and spouse, you must talk about creating workable, appropriate limits for these relationships. When you create a firm set of ground rules and make them clear to your in-laws, you take an important step toward avoiding conflict. For example, you might conclude that three days is the limit to how long in-laws may stay in your home. You might ask your in-laws not to bring candy for your children. Explain that, while you appreciate the thoughtful gesture, you have a no-sweets policy. With a firm set of rules, you will nip many problems in the bud. Finally, make sure your partner and marriage come first, and make sure that is clear through your words and actions.

The questions that follow will help you discuss your relationships with your families and agree upon the role your family members will play in your marriage and home life. Likewise, coming to an understanding about workable boundaries for extended family is a step in the direction of harmony and happiness in your marriage.

"The family is one of nature's masterpieces."

– George Santayana

Questions About Family

Are our parents married, divorced, separated, remarried, or deceased?

Partner 1: _____

_____

Partner 2: _____

_____

What are the best lessons our parents have taught us?

Partner 1: _____

_____

Partner 2: _____

_____

What advice about marriage will we take?

Partner 1: _____

_____

Partner 2: _____

_____

What advice won't we take?

Partner 1: _____

_____

Partner 2: _____

_____

What advice about child rearing we will take?

Partner 1: _____

_____

Partner 2: _____

_____

What advice won't we take?

Partner 1: _____

_____

Partner 2: _____

_____

Which family members have influenced our lives the most? How?

Partner 1: _____

_____

Partner 2: _____

_____

Who would we turn to for help if we were struggling financially?

Partner 1: _____

_____

Partner 2: _____

_____

How many times a year do we plan to visit our in-laws?

Partner 1: _____

_____

Partner 2: _____

_____

Can in-laws stop by our home unannounced?

Partner 1: _____

_____

Partner 2: _____

_____

How often will in-laws be allowed to visit us?

Partner 1: _____

_____

Partner 2: _____

_____

How many days will our in-laws stay when they visit?

Partner 1: _____

_____

Partner 2: _____

_____

Will they stay in our home or in a hotel?

Partner 1: _____

_____

Partner 2: _____

_____

What will we do if one of our family members is being rude or difficult?

Partner 1: _____

_____

Partner 2: _____

_____

Who will come first? Family or each other?

Partner 1: _____

_____

Partner 2: _____

_____

Are we comfortable with each other's parents?

Partner 1: _____

_____

Partner 2: _____

_____

Do we get along well with each other's siblings?

Partner 1: _____

_____

Partner 2: _____

_____

Describe our current relationships with our families.

Partner 1: _____

_____

Partner 2: _____

_____

Who would we like to become closer to?

Partner 1: _____

_____

Partner 2: _____

_____

How might we like to change our relationships with our families?

Partner 1: _____

_____

Partner 2: _____

_____

Who are our most helpful family members?

Partner 1: _____

_____

Partner 2: _____

_____

Is there anyone in our families we don't want to play a role in our lives?

Partner 1: _____

_____

Partner 2: _____

_____

Are there any family secrets or issues that may affect us?

Partner 1: _____

_____

Partner 2: _____

_____

How do we plan to take care of our aging family members?

Partner 1: _____

_____

Partner 2: _____

_____

Would we allow an aging parent to move in with us?

Partner 1: _____

_____

Partner 2: _____

_____

Would we send him or her to a nursing home?

Partner 1: _____

_____

Partner 2: _____

_____

Which holidays will we celebrate?

Partner 1: _____

_____

Partner 2: _____

_____

What holidays do we feel are most important to spend with family?

Partner 1: _____

_____

Partner 2: _____

_____

Will we exchange gifts with extended family during the holidays?

Partner 1: _____

_____

Partner 2: _____

_____

Which cultural traditions are important to our families?

Partner 1: _____

_____

Partner 2: _____

_____

Finances

The two of you were raised in households that likely took different approaches to money. As a result, you can expect to hold different, and sometimes contrasting, financial attitudes. Some people are natural savers, while others stretch each dollar to its limit. Some may feel safer with a budget; others may feel constricted by one. To see eye-to-eye on financial matters, you must discover what money symbolizes to you both, be it security, power, control, or freedom.

Money and finances consistently rank as the number one thing that married couples fight about; thus, it is extremely important to talk out your differences before the wedding. Ask your spouse how money played a role in his or her family and upbringing; it may clue you in to important attitudes about finances. For example, a person who appears cheap may have grown up with very little money and is thus careful about spending. This discussion will get to the root of your feelings toward spending and saving and help put you on the same financial page.

Discussing money can be scary for some couples, especially when you need to discuss debts. However, a discussion about the debts and assets you are both bringing into the marriage is imperative to managing your finances together. Make a list of what you owe, starting with high-interest debts like credit cards. Other debts might include medical bills, student loans, or car payments. It can be scary to realize how much you owe, but by assessing your debts and assets you know where you stand and where you need to go.

Once you have gone over your debts and assets and uncovered your attitudes about money, saving, and spending, you can discuss short- and long-term goals. Use these goals to come up with a budget and financial plan. Creating an effective budget will prevent you from living beyond your means, a major threat to the stability of your relationship.

Use the questions in this chapter to have a frank discussion about your financial attitudes, expectations, and goals. You'll be able to prevent many stressful money issues — and avoid the number one source of conflict in marriage!

"Who, being loved, is poor?"

– Oscar Wilde

Questions About Finances

How much income do we take home each year?

Partner 1: _____

_____

Partner 2: _____

_____

How much do we hope to make in 5 years? 10 years? 20 years?

Partner 1: _____

_____

Partner 2: _____

_____

Do we make enough right now to cover our expenses?

Partner 1: _____

_____

Partner 2: _____

_____

How much should we put aside from each paycheck for savings?

Partner 1: _____

_____

Partner 2: _____

_____

What savings will we create? Vacation fund? Children's college fund?

Partner 1: _____

_____

Partner 2: _____

_____

What will we invest in? Stocks? Mutual funds?

Partner 1: _____

_____

Partner 2: _____

_____

Who will research and make investment decisions?

Partner 1: _____

_____

Partner 2: _____

_____

Will we consult a financial planner?

Partner 1: _____

_____

Partner 2: _____

_____

How much outstanding debt does each of us have?

Partner 1: _____

_____

Partner 2: _____

_____

How do we plan to tackle our debts?

Partner 1: _____

_____

Partner 2: _____

_____

Does either of us have a large savings or trust?

Partner 1: _____

_____

Partner 2: _____

_____

Will we continue to let it grow or use it as a down payment on a house?

Partner 1: _____

_____

Partner 2: _____

_____

Do we know our credit scores?

Partner 1: _____

_____

Partner 2: _____

_____

Does either of us need to better our credit? How will we do this?

Partner 1: _____

_____

Partner 2: _____

_____

What financial mistakes have we made in the past and what did we learn?

Partner 1: _____

_____

Partner 2: _____

_____

How will we deal with it if one person makes more money than the other?

Partner 1: _____

_____

Partner 2: _____

_____

Will that person be allowed more decision-making power?

Partner 1: _____

_____

Partner 2: _____

_____

Will we create a monthly budget?

Partner 1: _____

_____

Partner 2: _____

_____

What will we splurge on?

Partner 1: _____

_____

Partner 2: _____

_____

Where should we cut back on our spending?

Partner 1: _____

_____

Partner 2: _____

_____

What are some easy ways we might save more money each month?

Partner 1: _____

_____

Partner 2: _____

_____

What motivates us to save?

Partner 1: _____

_____

Partner 2: _____

_____

What are some of our short-term financial goals?

Partner 1: _____

_____

Partner 2: _____

_____

What are some of our long-term financial goals?

Partner 1: _____

_____

Partner 2: _____

_____

How often will we revisit and reevaluate our goals?

Partner 1: _____

_____

Partner 2: _____

_____

Will we have money set aside for emergencies? How much?

Partner 1: _____

_____

Partner 2: _____

_____

Who will be responsible for paying the bills every month?

Partner 1: _____

_____

Partner 2: _____

_____

Will we have one joint account, separate accounts, or a combination?

Partner 1: _____

_____

Partner 2: _____

_____

What kinds of purchases will we make together?

Partner 1: _____

_____

Partner 2: _____

_____

What purchases will we consult each other about?

Partner 1: _____

_____

Partner 2: _____

_____

Will we be obligated to tell each other when we buy something new?

Partner 1: _____

_____

Partner 2: _____

_____

Will we each get discretionary money to spend as we like?

Partner 1: _____

_____

Partner 2: _____

_____

What are some large purchases we will make in the first year of marriage?

Partner 1: _____

_____

Partner 2: _____

_____

Do we have different or similar spending and saving styles?

Partner 1: _____

_____

Partner 2: _____

_____

Describe our spending style as a couple. Impulsive? Thrifty?

Partner 1: _____

_____

Partner 2: _____

_____

What are areas where we will need to compromise?

Partner 1: _____

_____

Partner 2: _____

_____

Do either of us have bad spending habits?

Partner 1: _____

_____

Partner 2: _____

_____

Are there incidents from our pasts that currently influence our finances?

Partner 1: _____

_____

Partner 2: _____

_____

What will be our biggest challenge with money in this marriage?

Partner 1: _____

_____

Partner 2: _____

_____

Are we into trends? Do we look for bargains or sales?

Partner 1: _____

_____

Partner 2: _____

_____

Will we give money to any charitable organizations? Which ones?

Partner 1: _____

_____

Partner 2: _____

_____

Who will prepare our taxes?

Partner 1: _____

_____

Partner 2: _____

_____

Will we save our tax return? Or what might we spend it on?

Partner 1: _____

_____

Partner 2: _____

_____

What would we do if we were unexpectedly left a large sum of money?

Partner 1: _____

_____

Partner 2: _____

_____

If times got tough, what would we eliminate from our spending?

Partner 1: _____

_____

Partner 2: _____

_____

Who might we turn to for help?

Partner 1: _____

_____

Partner 2: _____

_____

When will we draft our wills? Is it important to us to plan for our estate?

Partner 1: _____

_____

Partner 2: _____

_____

Are we worried about identity theft? How can we prevent it?

Partner 1: _____

_____

Partner 2: _____

_____

Do the ways we were raised influence the way we spend and save?

Partner 1: _____

_____

Partner 2: _____

_____

Who is more responsible with money, and why?

Partner 1: _____

_____

Partner 2: _____

_____

WORK & CAREER

We spend almost half of our week working, be it office time, overtime, or just the daily commute to and from work. For some people, their jobs are necessary evils, just a means to a paycheck and financial stability. Others feel fulfilled with their jobs, or perhaps view them as a stepping stone on a career path. A lucky few have found their dream jobs and love what they do. No matter how you and your partner feel about your current occupations, it is important to recognize the role work and career will play in your marriage.

Work and work-related stress can often find its way home and negatively affect a relationship. Be mindful of bringing too much work home with you, both literally and figuratively. The goal for your marriage is to find a happy medium between work and home life so that one does not outweigh the other. Naturally, you need to work to support yourselves and achieve your goals, but always keep in mind that your relationship is your most important job. Talk about how you can find solutions, such as the possibility of one of you working a compressed schedule.

It is also valuable to chat about your career hopes and goals, as well as how you can support one another in these endeavors. It is important to honor and validate your partner's hopes, dreams, and hidden talents. For instance, if your wife wants to get a master's degree, help her make it a reality. Remind her how intelligent she is on a regular basis. Encourage your spouse to talk about his or her passions. Give gentle nudges when he or she needs it. Assure your spouse you are there for support. By recognizing hopes and talents you are appreciating the shining star within your partner.

The following questions will get you talking about your jobs, career goals, and hopes for the future. This conversation will also help you discover the best ways to balance your commitments to work, home, and your relationship.

"And think not you can direct the course of love, for love, if it finds you worthy, directs your course."

– Kahlil Gibran

Questions About Work & Career

Do we both enjoy our jobs? What do we enjoy the most?

Partner 1: _____

_____

Partner 2: _____

_____

What are our greatest grievances about our jobs?

Partner 1: _____

_____

Partner 2: _____

_____

What are our individual career goals for the next 5 years? 10 years?

Partner 1: _____

_____

Partner 2: _____

_____

What are our individual career goals for the next 10 years?

Partner 1: _____

_____

Partner 2: _____

_____

Do we plan on staying in our fields?

Partner 1: _____

_____

Partner 2: _____

_____

What are our work hours?

Partner 1: _____

_____

Partner 2: _____

_____

How much time do we put into work after-hours?

Partner 1: _____

_____

Partner 2: _____

_____

How much work do we bring home with us?

Partner 1: _____

_____

Partner 2: _____

_____

Do our jobs make us feel stressed out?

Partner 1: _____

_____

Partner 2: _____

_____

Does stress from work affect our relationship?

Partner 1: _____

_____

Partner 2: _____

_____

Does one or both of us work too much?

Partner 1: _____

_____

Partner 2: _____

_____

Do we both plan to always work full-time?

Partner 1: _____

_____

Partner 2: _____

_____

Under what circumstances might one of us become strictly a homemaker?

Partner 1: _____

_____

Partner 2: _____

_____

Might one of us work from home? Do we have space for a home office?

Partner 1: _____

_____

Partner 2: _____

_____

Do we feel we both support each other's career goals?

Partner 1: _____

_____

Partner 2: _____

_____

How ambitious are we as a couple? Could we be more ambitious?

Partner 1: _____

_____

Partner 2: _____

_____

Would we want to work together if given the opportunity?

Partner 1: _____

_____

Partner 2: _____

_____

Will we attend office parties and events together?

Partner 1: _____

_____

Partner 2: _____

_____

Is it OK if one of us does not want to attend?

Partner 1: _____

_____

Partner 2: _____

_____

Does either of us plan to go back to school at any time?

Partner 1: _____

_____

Partner 2: _____

_____

Will it affect us if one of us has a more prestigious job than the other?

Partner 1: _____

_____

Partner 2: _____

_____

How will we feel if one of us has to travel frequently for work?

Partner 1: _____

_____

Partner 2: _____

_____

What are our dream jobs?

Partner 1: _____

_____

Partner 2: _____

_____

Are our dream jobs attainable?

Partner 1: _____

_____

Partner 2: _____

_____

What measures will we take to get our dream jobs?

Partner 1: _____

_____

Partner 2: _____

_____

Would we prefer to make a lot of money at jobs we hated,
or a little money at jobs we loved?

Partner 1: _____

_____

Partner 2: _____

_____

Do we receive good benefits from our current workplaces?

Partner 1: _____

_____

Partner 2: _____

_____

Are we offered 401(k)s or other ways to save for retirement at work?

Partner 1: _____

_____

Partner 2: _____

_____

How have we begun planning for retirement?

Partner 1: _____

_____

Partner 2: _____

_____

When do we want to retire?

Partner 1: _____

_____

Partner 2: _____

_____

HEALTH

You surely know a great deal about each other: perhaps more than even lifelong friends or family members do. You probably know everything from favorite flavors of ice cream to deep, dark secrets. However, you may not be aware of some of each other's health risks, concerns, and needs — knowledge that is crucially important for a married couple.

It is extremely important to discuss short-term and long-term health concerns, such as high blood pressure, cancer, and heart disease. One or both of you may be at risk because of family history, weight, diet, or other factors. Once you have an understanding of these risks, you will know what to look out for and how to adapt your married lifestyle to avoid health problems. For instance, you may decide, as a team, to quit smoking or to tackle other unhealthy habits. It's imperative to be conscious of your choices, and also to know how you will support each other during any kind of illness — even a common cold.

Another health issue to discuss as a couple is exercise. Exercise affects both physical health and your marital happiness. Millions of people are unhappy with their appearance, and it severely affects their self-esteem and thus, their relationships.

The American Council on Exercise reports that exercise affects both the mind and body. It improves muscle tone, endurance, and cardiovascular health. Additionally, studies have shown that regular exercise leads to a happier, more robust sex life. The *Electronic Journal of Human Sexuality* concluded that individuals who exercise regularly perceive themselves as more desirable and experience greater levels of sexual satisfaction. Exercise helps you feel happier with your appearance, making you more excited about intimacy. You will find that if you work out, you will have more sexual energy than ever before.

You will want to talk about how happy (or unhappy) you are with your levels of activity, frequency of exercise, eating habits, and more. To stay in good physical shape and address any hereditary health issues, start by discussing the questions in this chapter. Lucky for you, being healthy is always easier when you have a partner!

"Laugh as much as you breathe
and love as long as you live."

— Anonymous

Questions About Health

Do we have adequate health care?

Partner 1: _____

_____

Partner 2: _____

_____

Are there health risks in our families that we should consider?

Partner 1: _____

_____

Partner 2: _____

_____

Are any diseases prevalent in our families?

Partner 1: _____

_____

Partner 2: _____

_____

How will we help out when one of us gets sick?

Partner 1: _____

_____

Partner 2: _____

_____

Are we in good physical shape?

Partner 1: _____

_____

Partner 2: _____

_____

Are we both satisfied with our weight and appearance?

Partner 1: _____

_____

Partner 2: _____

_____

What is each of our favorite things about our bodies?

Partner 1: _____

_____

Partner 2: _____

_____

What are our least favorite things? Can we change them?

Partner 1: _____

_____

Partner 2: _____

_____

How often do we work out?

Partner 1: _____

_____

Partner 2: _____

_____

Should we be exercising more?

Partner 1: _____

_____

Partner 2: _____

_____

How often would we like to work out ideally?

Partner 1: _____

_____

Partner 2: _____

_____

Do we both feel supported in these endeavors?

Partner 1: _____

_____

Partner 2: _____

_____

Do we prefer to exercise together?

Partner 1: _____

_____

Partner 2: _____

_____

How will we get exercise? Join a gym? Take walks together? Ride bikes?

Partner 1: _____

_____

Partner 2: _____

_____

Will we still be just as much in love if one of us gains weight?

Partner 1: _____

_____

Partner 2: _____

_____

How do we plan to stay healthy as we age?

Partner 1: _____

_____

Partner 2: _____

_____

Do we consider ourselves healthy eaters?

Partner 1: _____

_____

Partner 2: _____

_____

Will we diet together?

Partner 1: _____

_____

Partner 2: _____

_____

Would either of us consider plastic surgery? What kind?

Partner 1: _____

_____

Partner 2: _____

_____

Do either of us snore?

Partner 1: _____

_____

Partner 2: _____

_____

Are either of us on antidepressants?

Partner 1: _____

_____

Partner 2: _____

_____

Do either of us see or need to see a counselor? What are the reasons?

Partner 1: _____

_____

Partner 2: _____

_____

Are there other health habits that are concerning, such as smoking?

Partner 1: _____

_____

Partner 2: _____

_____

How many nights a week do we drink alcohol?

Partner 1: _____

_____

Partner 2: _____

_____

Would it be acceptable if one of us had one drink every day?

Partner 1: _____

_____

Partner 2: _____

_____

Are there any major lifestyle changes we should make to be healthier?

Partner 1: _____

_____

Partner 2: _____

_____

Will it be easier or harder to be healthy as a married couple?

Partner 1: _____

_____

Partner 2: _____

_____

Do we plan to relax more after we are married?

Partner 1: _____

_____

Partner 2: _____

_____

Would you get your spouse's name tattooed on your body?

Partner 1: _____

_____

Partner 2: _____

_____

If yes, where?

Partner 1: _____

_____

Partner 2: _____

_____

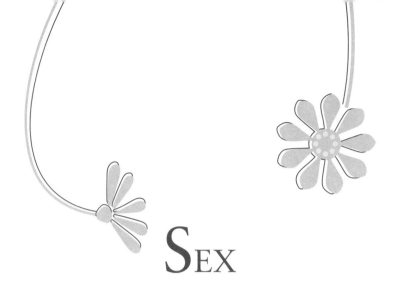

Sex

It is a fact that sex can bring you closer together or drive you apart. The key to a wonderful sex life begins — like all the topics in this book — with communication. Talking openly about sex can actually enrich your sex life and keep it passionate. Discussing your wants, needs, desires, and sexual fantasies can be enlightening, liberating, and even a turn-on! Of course, it can also be intimidating to talk about sex. When you share, keep in mind that you are also best friends. Be sensitive to each other's feelings, but don't hold back. You're not discussing what is lacking, only what you might gain together. Remember that sex provides mutual pleasure, shows meaningful physical and emotional closeness, and is a way to show your partner you are in tune with his or her needs.

A sex life that meets both partners' needs is vital to your happiness as a couple. Beyond being an expression of your deepest love, sex will improve all areas of your lives. Sex reduces the risk of cancer, disease, heart attack, and stroke. Having a great marital sex life also gives you confidence, relaxes you, clears your mind, improves your ability to focus, and even reduces depression.

As you discuss the questions in this chapter, it is important to understand that men and women view sex very differently. Men are turned on by visual cues and often view sex as the main route to connect. Women, on the other hand, need to be aroused physically or psychologically and are driven by a desire for emotional connection. Women respond to subtler cues, such as an affectionate touch, romantic meal, or even an intimate conversation.

Perhaps you have always had an explosive sexual connection. Perhaps you are best friends first and lovers second. Not every couple has sex every day, or even every week. Your levels of desire won't always be the same. Likewise, no matter what kind of sex life you have now, know that your sex drives will wax and wane throughout the course of your marriage. The following questions will help you talk openly about your expectations for your sex life (and perhaps even get you in the mood for love).

"Love is an irresistible desire to be
irresistibly desired."

– Robert Frost

Questions About Sex

How would we describe our sex life?

Partner 1: _____

_____

Partner 2: _____

_____

Describe our favorite sexual experience together.

Partner 1: _____

_____

Partner 2: _____

_____

Describe our favorite part of our sex life.

Partner 1: _____

_____

Partner 2: _____

_____

How do we get in the mood?

Partner 1: _____

_____

Partner 2: _____

_____

What takes us out of the mood?

Partner 1: _____

_____

Partner 2: _____

_____

What is the craziest place we have had sex?

Partner 1: _____

_____

Partner 2: _____

_____

What music do we like to have playing during sex?

Partner 1: _____

_____

Partner 2: _____

_____

What is our favorite time of day to have sex?

Partner 1: _____

_____

Partner 2: _____

_____

Are we affectionate often enough outside of sex?

Partner 1: _____

_____

Partner 2: _____

_____

Are we satisfied with how often we make love?

Partner 1: _____

_____

Partner 2: _____

_____

Are we on the same page sexually?

Partner 1: _____

_____

Partner 2: _____

_____

Do we have a deep connection, or is it something we have to work on?

Partner 1: _____

_____

Partner 2: _____

_____

What will we do if one of us wants sex more often than the other?

Partner 1: _____

_____

Partner 2: _____

_____

How will we work on keeping our sex life interesting over a lifetime?

Partner 1: _____

_____

Partner 2: _____

_____

Are we both comfortable sharing our sexual wants and needs?

Partner 1: _____

_____

Partner 2: _____

_____

Do we feel comfortable sharing our most private fantasies?

Partner 1: _____

_____

Partner 2: _____

_____

Are there wishes or fantasies we've held back?

Partner 1: _____

_____

Partner 2: _____

_____

Is our sex life very spontaneous or do we have a routine?

Partner 1: _____

_____

Partner 2: _____

_____

How can we spice up our sex life in the future?

Partner 1: _____

_____

Partner 2: _____

_____

What would we do if one of us was attracted to someone else?

Partner 1: _____

_____

Partner 2: _____

_____

If our sex life slows down, does that mean there is a problem?

Partner 1: _____

_____

Partner 2: _____

_____

What will we do if we hit a sexual rut?

Partner 1: _____

_____

Partner 2: _____

_____

How do we feel about watching or owning pornography?

Partner 1: _____

_____

Partner 2: _____

_____

How do we feel about incorporating sex toys?

Partner 1: _____

_____

Partner 2: _____

_____

How do we feel about incorporating sexual aids, such as Viagra?

Partner 1: _____

_____

Partner 2: _____

_____

Would we consider seeing a counselor if our sex life was struggling?

Partner 1: _____

_____

Partner 2: _____

_____

Do we feel we say "I love you" often enough?

Partner 1: _____

_____

Partner 2: _____

_____

Do we trust each other completely when we're apart?

Partner 1: _____

_____

Partner 2: _____

_____

Are either of us attracted to any celebrities?

Partner 1: _____

_____

Partner 2: _____

_____

One thing that would really improve our sex life:

Partner 1: _____

_____

Partner 2: _____

_____

Our Social Life

Many couples get married and drop out of the social scene completely. While you are no doubt looking forward to being newlyweds, you want to discuss the best ways to make time for each other and friends after you're married. While it is important to cultivate an active social life as a pair, it is equally important to encourage each other to nurture independent friendships.

Not only is having great friends a lot of fun, but studies have consistently demonstrated the health benefits of close friendships. Reliable friendships are a natural stress-reducer, can lengthen your lifespan, and can reduce the incidence of depression and insomnia. Just as solidarity with your mate will help you weather the tough times, having a strong, supportive network of friends will help you both when you are struggling. French writer Marcel Proust wisely wrote, "Let us be grateful to people who make us happy, they are the charming gardeners who make our souls blossom."

Additionally, an active social life keeps you growing as a couple. Friends can help you discover new interests and passions you might not have considered otherwise. Both single friends and other married couples can recommend or introduce you to new eateries, activities, organizations, and pastimes. Openness, flexibility, and a sense of adventure are keys to having a healthy social life as a couple.

The idea is to maintain a balance between your social life as a pair and your independent friendships. You can do this by talking about your comfort levels. For instance, is your husband comfortable with all your friendships, or is there one that makes him feel uneasy? Along the same lines, is there something you can do to put your wife at ease when you plan a guys' night out? Finally, are you making time to be together often enough? Naturally, you're both busy people, but scheduling a movie night or an evening out together is vital. It is helpful to check in with each other to make sure you are both maintaining a healthy balance within your social lives.

Talk through the questions in this chapter to get each other's perspectives on your time together and the quality of your friendships. You will reap the rewards of a happy and healthy marital social life.

"Love is the greatest refreshment in life."

– Pablo Picasso

Questions About Our Social Life

How will being married affect the amount of time we spend with friends?

Partner 1: _____

_____

Partner 2: _____

_____

Do we go on enough dates, just the two of us?

Partner 1: _____

_____

Partner 2: _____

_____

How often should we plan date nights once we're married?

Partner 1: _____

_____

Partner 2: _____

_____

What kinds of dates would we like to plan?

Partner 1: _____

_____

Partner 2: _____

_____

Do we spend too much time with our friends? Not enough?

Partner 1: _____

_____

Partner 2: _____

_____

What restaurant or hangout spot would we like to try?

Partner 1: _____

_____

Partner 2: _____

_____

What kinds of activities do we both like?

Partner 1: _____

_____

Partner 2: _____

_____

Are there activities that one of us enjoys but the other can't stand?

Partner 1: _____

_____

Partner 2: _____

_____

Would we try something we don't like because the other person enjoys it?

Partner 1: _____

_____

Partner 2: _____

_____

Do we encourage each other to spend time independently? How often?

Partner 1: _____

_____

Partner 2: _____

_____

Are we equally comfortable with one person going out alone?

Partner 1: _____

_____

Partner 2: _____

_____

Does one of us need more alone time than the other?

Partner 1: _____

_____

Partner 2: _____

_____

Do we respect the need for space?

Partner 1: _____

_____

Partner 2: _____

_____

Who are our favorite friends to spend time with?

Partner 1: _____

_____

Partner 2: _____

_____

Who are our favorite couples to spend time with?

Partner 1: _____

_____

Partner 2: _____

_____

Are we satisfied with the quality of our friendships?

Partner 1: _____

_____

Partner 2: _____

_____

Would we like to meet a new social circle?

Partner 1: _____

_____

Partner 2: _____

_____

How will we make friends with couples who have similar interests as us?

Partner 1: _____

_____

Partner 2: _____

_____

Do we both get along with each other's friends?

Partner 1: _____

_____

Partner 2: _____

_____

Is there a friendship that is especially wonderful to our relationship?

Partner 1: _____

_____

Partner 2: _____

_____

Is there a friendship that is harmful to our relationship?

Partner 1: _____
_____

Partner 2: _____
_____

Are there ex-boyfriends or ex-girlfriends still in our lives?

Partner 1: _____
_____

Partner 2: _____
_____

How do we feel about this?

Partner 1: _____
_____

Partner 2: _____
_____

What kinds of social or community events would we like to engage in?

Partner 1: _____
_____

Partner 2: _____
_____

Is there a class we want to take together?

Partner 1: _____
_____

Partner 2: _____
_____

Is there a club or organization we could join together?

Partner 1: _____

_____

Partner 2: _____

_____

How do we imagine our social life after marriage?

Partner 1: _____

_____

Partner 2: _____

_____

Do we feel either of us gets out of control when we go out?

Partner 1: _____

_____

Partner 2: _____

_____

If so, how can we deal with that?

Partner 1: _____

_____

Partner 2: _____

_____

Do we have the same social style?

Partner 1: _____

_____

Partner 2: _____

_____

Do we prefer to go out or stay in?

Partner 1: _____

_____

Partner 2: _____

_____

Do we enjoy the same social events?

Partner 1: _____

_____

Partner 2: _____

_____

What is our perfect Saturday night?

Partner 1: _____

_____

Partner 2: _____

_____

Do we approve of girls' and guys' nights out? How often?

Partner 1: _____

_____

Partner 2: _____

_____

If one of us was invited to a wild party, would he or she be allowed to go?

Partner 1: _____

_____

Partner 2: _____

_____

Do we prefer to host a party or attend a party?

Partner 1: _____

_____

Partner 2: _____

_____

Are there any parties we plan to throw in the next year?

Partner 1: _____

_____

Partner 2: _____

_____

Do we prefer group dates or just us two?

Partner 1: _____

_____

Partner 2: _____

_____

Are we more homebodies or party animals?

Partner 1: _____

_____

Partner 2: _____

_____

How can we change our social life for the better?

Partner 1: _____

_____

Partner 2: _____

_____

Morals & Ethics

American painter Walter Anderson once said, "We're never so vulnerable than when we trust someone — but paradoxically, if we cannot trust, neither can we find love or joy." Trust will be an integral part of your successful marriage. It is the foundation of intimacy, the doorway to commitment. Trust means having confidence that you will treat each other fairly, honestly, and responsibly. Trust takes years to build, and means different things to different couples. Some couples build trust through traveling and having extraordinary experiences together; others build trust through fidelity; still others built trust by showing each other sides of themselves that no one else may know.

The reality about trust is that it is delicate — easy to break and very difficult to rebuild. It can be damaged in mere moments and can take months, or years, to repair.

If you want to enjoy a healthy and happy marriage, you

must learn two things: to trust your partner and to be trustworthy yourself. The questions in this chapter present specific situations when a tough decision would need to be made. People do not have the exact same concepts of integrity, so these questions will help you gauge your definitions of right and wrong, as well as the gray area in-between. For instance, one of you may feel it is necessary to share everything with your spouse. On the contrary, the other person may feel there are circumstances where it is acceptable and right to keep some things private, such as information shared by a friend in confidence. You will learn some vital things about each other's ethics in this chapter.

Don't get upset if you don't completely agree on every question. Not every decision is cut and dry; each situation has stipulations and conditions that should be discussed. Thankfully, this is a great opportunity to air some differences you may have and to get on the same page on what is expected.

By tackling these tricky examples, you will be getting one step closer to the strong foundation of trust your marriage will need.

"Do the right thing.
It will gratify some people and astonish the rest."

— Mark Twain

Questions About Morals & Ethics

If you found a wallet with $100 in it, would you keep the money? Would you take the time to return the wallet?

Partner 1: _____

_____

Partner 2: _____

_____

If you received an email from an ex-boyfriend or ex-girlfriend, would you tell your partner?

Partner 1: _____

_____

Partner 2: _____

_____

If you saw a friend's husband or wife out with a member of the opposite sex, would you tell your friend? What would you say?

Partner 1: _____

_____

Partner 2: _____

_____

Do you think it's acceptable to lie on your taxes? Under what circumstances would it be OK?

Partner 1: _____

_____

Partner 2: _____

_____

If a friend told you something in confidence, would you tell your spouse?

Partner 1: _____

_____

Partner 2: _____

_____

Under what circumstances?

Partner 1: _____

_____

Partner 2: _____

_____

Would you park in a handicap parking spot if it was more convenient?

Partner 1: _____

_____

Partner 2: _____

_____

If you got too much change back on a purchase, would you tell the clerk?

Partner 1: _____

_____

Partner 2: _____

_____

Would you flirt your way out of a traffic ticket?

Partner 1: _____

_____

Partner 2: _____

_____

Are white lies OK in a relationship?

Partner 1: _____

_____

Partner 2: _____

_____

Would you support a friend who wanted to have an abortion?

Partner 1: _____

_____

Partner 2: _____

_____

Would you take credit for a coworker's work to get a big promotion?

Partner 1: _____

_____

Partner 2: _____

_____

Do you condone recreational drug use?

Partner 1: _____

_____

Partner 2: _____

_____

Have either of you ever tried drugs? Which ones?

Partner 1: _____

_____

Partner 2: _____

_____

Is there ever such a thing as innocent flirting?

Partner 1: _____

_____

Partner 2: _____

_____

Would you report a shoplifter? Why or why not?

Partner 1: _____

_____

Partner 2: _____

_____

How would we deal with it if an employer was flirting with one of us?

Partner 1: _____

_____

Partner 2: _____

_____

Would you drive through a red light if no other cars were around?

Partner 1: _____

_____

Partner 2: _____

_____

Would you shoot someone if they were breaking into your home?

Partner 1: _____

_____

Partner 2: _____

_____

If you hit a parked car and no one saw, would you leave a note?

Partner 1: _____

_____

Partner 2: _____

_____

What would you do if a nice gift was mistakenly delivered to your home?

Partner 1: _____

_____

Partner 2: _____

_____

How would we react if a friend of ours hit on one of us?

Partner 1: _____

_____

Partner 2: _____

_____

Would we confront the friend? Would we end this friendship?

Partner 1: _____

_____

Partner 2: _____

_____

If you bought an expensive item, would you hide it from your partner?

Partner 1: _____

_____

Partner 2: _____

_____

If you kissed someone else, would you come clean?

Partner 1: _____

_____

Partner 2: _____

_____

If you lost your wedding band, would you tell your partner?

Partner 1: _____

_____

Partner 2: _____

_____

How long does it take to restore trust once it has been broken?

Partner 1: _____

_____

Partner 2: _____

_____

Are there any incidents that are unforgiveable?

Partner 1: _____

_____

Partner 2: _____

_____

TRAVEL

Consider the wisdom of the Chinese proverb that says, "Vacations are not about 'getting away' — but about getting in 'touch.'" Taking a vacation is a perfect way to rejuvenate, reconnect, and make lifelong memories as a married couple.

Best of all, a change of scenery almost always cultivates romance. According to a survey conducted by the travel company Expedia, 60 percent of couples feel that time away with their partners improves their relationships. Getting away doesn't have to take lots of money or time — a night spent in a local hotel or a weekend devoted to exploring a nearby destination can be just as significant as an exotic beach vacation. Think of a special place or landmark you would like to see; make sure you include both people in the planning process. Whether you spend the day in wine country, take a road trip to the Grand Canyon, or tour the Greek Isles, realize that it doesn't really matter where you go — just that you are on a journey together.

Vacationing takes planning — for more than just the place and your itinerary. Trips can be very expensive, and many couples budget and save up for vacations just as they would for a new car or a down payment on a home. It is valuable to talk to your partner about how often you want to travel, where you might like to go, what time of year, and how you will budget for trips. Consider both weekend jaunts and large trips. Consider what your dream vacation might be. Is it the same for both of you? Some people like to plan an itinerary packed with activities and sightseeing. Others prefer to relax completely. "Getting away" doesn't always mean the same thing to both people.

The questions in this chapter will help you understand each other's hopes for future travel plans, including your honeymoon and all the years to come.

"To get the full value of joy
you must have someone to divide it with."

— Mark Twain

Questions About Travel

What is our favorite vacation we've taken together?

Partner 1: _____

_____

Partner 2: _____

_____

What are three domestic cities we'd like to visit?

Partner 1: _____

_____

Partner 2: _____

_____

What are three foreign countries we'd like to visit?

Partner 1: _____

_____

Partner 2: _____

_____

What famous landmark would we like to visit?

Partner 1: _____

_____

Partner 2: _____

_____

What has been the most spontaneous vacation we've taken together?

Partner 1: _____

_____

Partner 2: _____

_____

What was the most disastrous vacation we've taken together?

Partner 1: _____

_____

Partner 2: _____

_____

Describe a type of trip we are interested in taking in the future.

Partner 1: _____

_____

Partner 2: _____

_____

Describe a place we agree we never want to visit. Why?

Partner 1: _____

_____

Partner 2: _____

_____

Will we set money aside for vacations?

Partner 1: _____

_____

Partner 2: _____

_____

How often do we plan to take vacations?

Partner 1: _____

_____

Partner 2: _____

_____

Is travel equally important to both of us?

Partner 1: _____

_____

Partner 2: _____

_____

Is one of us more of a homebody or more of an adventurer?

Partner 1: _____

_____

Partner 2: _____

_____

Do we enjoy the same kinds of vacations?

Partner 1: _____

_____

Partner 2: _____

_____

What do we seek to get out of vacationing?

Partner 1: _____

_____

Partner 2: _____

_____

Do we have the same kind of traveling style?

Partner 1: _____

_____

Partner 2: _____

_____

When we travel, do we like to sightsee or relax?

Partner 1: _____

_____

Partner 2: _____

_____

Would we be interested in taking a cruise?

Partner 1: _____

_____

Partner 2: _____

_____

Will we sacrifice luxury for price, such as staying in a hostel versus a resort?

Partner 1: _____

_____

Partner 2: _____

_____

Who plans our vacations? Will we be equally involved in the planning?

Partner 1: _____

_____

Partner 2: _____

_____

Do we prefer to travel alone, with family, or with friends?

Partner 1: _____

_____

Partner 2: _____

_____

Which friends would we like to travel with?

Partner 1: _____

_____

Partner 2: _____

_____

Who would we like to avoid traveling with?

Partner 1: _____

_____

Partner 2: _____

_____

What would we do if our luggage was lost while on a week-long trip?

Partner 1: _____

_____

Partner 2: _____

_____

How would we react if we were pickpocketed while on vacation?

Partner 1: _____

_____

Partner 2: _____

_____

What is one thing we learned about us as a couple from traveling?

Partner 1: _____

_____

Partner 2: _____

_____

What is our dream vacation?

Partner 1: _____

_____

Partner 2: _____

_____

How long would we be gone? About how much would it cost?

Partner 1: _____

_____

Partner 2: _____

_____

Do we agree on where to go for our honeymoon?

Partner 1: _____

_____

Partner 2: _____

_____

Do we want a relaxing honeymoon or one full of activities?

Partner 1: _____

_____

Partner 2: _____

_____

What types of activities do we want to do on our honeymoon?

Partner 1: _____

_____

Partner 2: _____

_____

Handling Conflict

People fight in very different ways. Some people have hot tempers that flare up quickly, while others shut down completely during an argument. Some people are pleasers, quick to take blame just to end a disagreement, while others strive to always be right. None of these behaviors is healthy for your marriage; thus, it is extremely important to talk about your "fighting styles" and the ways you plan to resolve conflict.

The German writer Goethe once said, "It is sometimes essential for a husband and a wife to quarrel — they get to know each other better." It is true that some conflict is actually healthy for your marriage. Conflict gives both people a chance to express their thoughts and feelings and shows you are both engaged in the relationship. In fact, marriages where the couple does not fight are often deeply troubled; problems that are not confronted can grow and escalate and cause distance.

Learning to navigate your way through a conflict will result in a loving, happy home. The questions in this chapter can help you identify issues that may cause conflict and how to deal with those times when you disagree. There will be instances when you may be able to simply say, "This is not very important to me," in the interest of ending an argument. Other times, you may both feel so strongly about an issue that it escalates into a full-blown fight. There are also, undoubtedly, issues that will become "no-compromise zones" — areas where one person is unwilling to compromise and it shouldn't be forced (political affiliation and religion are examples). Talking about these instances before the wedding will better prepare you for any conflict that arises.

Finally, these questions will help you discuss another skill crucial to the success of your marriage: forgiveness. Invariably, situations will arise where one of you will need to forgive or be forgiven. Practicing forgiveness will strengthen your union and help you foster trust, respect, fairness, and communication. Use the following questions to tackle the tricky subject of handling conflict.

"Love doesn't make the world go round.
Love is what makes the ride worthwhile."

— Franklin P. Jones

Questions About Handling Conflict

Do we express dissatisfaction in the same way or differently?

Partner 1: _____

_____

Partner 2: _____

_____

Do we wear our hearts on our sleeves or keep things bottled up inside?

Partner 1: _____

_____

Partner 2: _____

_____

What are the habitual things we disagree on?

Partner 1: _____

_____

Partner 2: _____

_____

What silly thing do we always disagree about?

Partner 1: _____

_____

Partner 2: _____

_____

How do we plan to handle topics we continuously disagree on?

Partner 1: _____

_____

Partner 2: _____

_____

Are there certain things one of us is not willing to compromise on?

Partner 1: _____

_____

Partner 2: _____

_____

What are the best ways we plan to deal with disagreements?

Partner 1: _____

_____

Partner 2: _____

_____

What tactics can we agree *never* to use during an argument?

Partner 1: _____

_____

Partner 2: _____

_____

Do we feel we both fight fair?

Partner 1: _____

_____

Partner 2: _____

_____

What do we feel constitutes "fighting dirty"?

Partner 1: _____

_____

Partner 2: _____

_____

Do we know each other's biggest pet peeves? Name a few.

Partner 1: _____

_____

Partner 2: _____

_____

Will we make an effort to avoid them?

Partner 1: _____

_____

Partner 2: _____

_____

Do we feel one of us is too sensitive? On which issues?

Partner 1: _____

_____

Partner 2: _____

_____

How flexible are we?

Partner 1: _____

_____

Partner 2: _____

_____

Is one of us more willing to give in for the sake of harmony than the other?

Partner 1: _____

_____

Partner 2: _____

_____

How will we cope after a fight? Does one of us prefer alone time?

Partner 1: _____

_____

Partner 2: _____

_____

How will we cool down after a heated argument?

Partner 1: _____

_____

Partner 2: _____

_____

Will we have "make-up sex"?

Partner 1: _____

_____

Partner 2: _____

_____

How long does it take us to get over a fight?

Partner 1: _____

_____

Partner 2: _____

_____

Do we withhold sex or affection when we are in an argument?

Partner 1: _____

_____

Partner 2: _____

_____

How will we react if we are late to an important event?

Partner 1: _____

_____

Partner 2: _____

_____

How will we react to an individual who is threatening our marriage?

Partner 1: _____

_____

Partner 2: _____

_____

Do we ever argue in public or embarrass our friends when we argue?

Partner 1: _____

_____

Partner 2: _____

_____

How forgiving are we? Is it hard or easy to forgive the other person?

Partner 1: _____

_____

Partner 2: _____

_____

Are there any occurrences that we consider unforgivable?

Partner 1: _____

_____

Partner 2: _____

_____

Do we both apologize when necessary?

Partner 1: _____

_____

Partner 2: _____

_____

What is our biggest obstacle to overcome in regards to conflict?

Partner 1: _____

_____

Partner 2: _____

_____

Would we consider marital counseling if we were struggling?

Partner 1: _____

_____

Partner 2: _____

_____

How do we plan to keep conflict in our marriage to a minimum?

Partner 1: _____

_____

Partner 2: _____

_____

Do we think some fighting is healthy? How much? How often?

Partner 1: _____

_____

Partner 2: _____

_____

TRUE OR FALSE

The true or false questions in this chapter are designed to get you talking about a variety of different feelings and outlooks on your relationship. Some will spark serious, insightful conversation while others will reveal important attitudes about and perceptions of your relationship. These types of conversations can help you nurture your relationship, create realistic expectations, build trust, and grow within your partnership.

As you go over these questions, be conscious of being very respectful of each other, even when you don't agree on a topic. It has been said that the goal in marriage is not to think alike, but to think together — aim for this when you go over these questions. Respect means working to understand your spouse's point of view because you believe it has value. Acknowledge that other opinions exist and are valid, even if you maintain your own point of view in the end.

Your upbringing, families, past friendships, and past relationships have all molded you into the kind of partner you are today. Through these types of exercises, you can better understand and love each other. Naturally, your marriage will be ever-evolving as you grow together and individually.

Happy couples create a safe environment in which to share their feelings, concerns, and issues. So, be respectful and open-minded about your answers during the following chapter. You may learn some fascinating things about your future spouse's perceptions and attitudes about your relationship!

"Couples who love each other tell each other
a thousand things without talking."

– Chinese proverb

True or False

I feel like I can ask my loved one anything.
Partner 1: ❏ True ❏ False   Partner 2: ❏ True ❏ False

I am grumpy in the morning.
Partner 1: ❏ True ❏ False   Partner 2: ❏ True ❏ False

I think I am better looking than my partner's last boyfriend/girlfriend.
Partner 1: ❏ True ❏ False   Partner 2: ❏ True ❏ False

I think my partner and I fight too much.
Partner 1: ❏ True ❏ False   Partner 2: ❏ True ❏ False

I think we fight about things that aren't important.
Partner 1: ❏ True ❏ False   Partner 2: ❏ True ❏ False

I wish we communicated better.
Partner 1: ❏ True ❏ False   Partner 2: ❏ True ❏ False

My partner spends too much time getting ready.
Partner 1: ❏ True ❏ False   Partner 2: ❏ True ❏ False

My partner owns certain clothing I wish I could throw out.
Partner 1: ❏ True ❏ False   Partner 2: ❏ True ❏ False

I believe in love at first sight.
Partner 1: ❏ True ❏ False   Partner 2: ❏ True ❏ False

I believe that opposites attract.
Partner 1: ❏ True ❏ False   Partner 2: ❏ True ❏ False

I do my share of household chores.

Partner 1: ❏ True ❏ False   Partner 2: ❏ True ❏ False

My partner gives me enough space when I have a bad day.

Partner 1: ❏ True ❏ False   Partner 2: ❏ True ❏ False

I have a hidden talent that my partner doesn't know about.

Partner 1: ❏ True ❏ False   Partner 2: ❏ True ❏ False

My partner makes me feel like the most important person in the world.

Partner 1: ❏ True ❏ False   Partner 2: ❏ True ❏ False

I have caught my partner looking at another man/woman.

Partner 1: ❏ True ❏ False   Partner 2: ❏ True ❏ False

My partner has a friend who flirts with him/her.

Partner 1: ❏ True ❏ False   Partner 2: ❏ True ❏ False

I think my partner is too flirty.

Partner 1: ❏ True ❏ False   Partner 2: ❏ True ❏ False

I trust my partner 100 percent.

Partner 1: ❏ True ❏ False   Partner 2: ❏ True ❏ False

I think my partner has attractive friends.

Partner 1: ❏ True ❏ False   Partner 2: ❏ True ❏ False

I would be fine if my partner went to a movie with a female/male friend.

Partner 1: ❏ True ❏ False   Partner 2: ❏ True ❏ False

My partner knows more about politics than me.

Partner 1: ❏ True ❏ False   Partner 2: ❏ True ❏ False

My partner knows more about sports than me.

Partner 1: ❏ True ❏ False   Partner 2: ❏ True ❏ False

If my partner gained 20 pounds, I would still find him/her as attractive.

Partner 1: ❏ True ❏ False   Partner 2: ❏ True ❏ False

I don't mind my partner's morning breath.

Partner 1: ❏ True ❏ False   Partner 2: ❏ True ❏ False

Sex is crucial to my happiness.

Partner 1: ❏ True ❏ False   Partner 2: ❏ True ❏ False

I would like to have sex twice as often.

Partner 1: ❏ True ❏ False   Partner 2: ❏ True ❏ False

I would go crazy if my partner was gone for more than a week.

Partner 1: ❏ True ❏ False   Partner 2: ❏ True ❏ False

My partner has a habit I can't stand.

Partner 1: ❏ True ❏ False   Partner 2: ❏ True ❏ False

I would like to get a cat or dog.

Partner 1: ❏ True ❏ False   Partner 2: ❏ True ❏ False

I want to have more than two kids.

Partner 1: ❏ True ❏ False   Partner 2: ❏ True ❏ False

I like how my partner smells.

Partner 1: ❏ True ❏ False   Partner 2: ❏ True ❏ False

I have an unfulfilled bedroom fantasy.

Partner 1: ❏ True ❏ False   Partner 2: ❏ True ❏ False

I watch X-rated movies when my partner isn't around.

Partner 1: ❏ True ❏ False   Partner 2: ❏ True ❏ False

I tell my parents details of our relationship.

Partner 1: ❏ True ❏ False   Partner 2: ❏ True ❏ False

My partner has a family member or friend I can't stand.

Partner 1: ❏ True ❏ False   Partner 2: ❏ True ❏ False

I believe in karma.

Partner 1: ❏ True ❏ False   Partner 2: ❏ True ❏ False

I believe in the statement "everything happens for a reason."

Partner 1: ❏ True ❏ False   Partner 2: ❏ True ❏ False

If I was fired, my partner is the first person I would tell.

Partner 1: ❏ True ❏ False   Partner 2: ❏ True ❏ False

I think my partner is a good listener.

Partner 1: ❏ True ❏ False   Partner 2: ❏ True ❏ False

I think my partner is very understanding.

Partner 1: ❏ True ❏ False   Partner 2: ❏ True ❏ False

I have gone skinny-dipping.

Partner 1: ❏ True ❏ False   Partner 2: ❏ True ❏ False

I have spent a night in jail.

Partner 1: ❏ True ❏ False   Partner 2: ❏ True ❏ False

I believe in aliens.

Partner 1: ❏ True ❏ False   Partner 2: ❏ True ❏ False

I believe in ghosts.

Partner 1: ❏ True ❏ False   Partner 2: ❏ True ❏ False

I believe that people who cheat should get a second chance.

Partner 1: ❏ True ❏ False   Partner 2: ❏ True ❏ False

I have given someone a black eye.

Partner 1: ❏ True ❏ False   Partner 2: ❏ True ❏ False

I have been to a strip club.

Partner 1: ❏ True ❏ False   Partner 2: ❏ True ❏ False

I believe in God.

Partner 1: ❏ True ❏ False   Partner 2: ❏ True ❏ False

I have had a one-night stand.

Partner 1: ❏ True ❏ False   Partner 2: ❏ True ❏ False

I think it is OK to fight in public.

Partner 1: ❏ True ❏ False   Partner 2: ❏ True ❏ False

I have been in a car accident.

Partner 1: ❑ True ❑ False   Partner 2: ❑ True ❑ False

My partner has gotten drunk and embarrassed me.

Partner 1: ❑ True ❑ False   Partner 2: ❑ True ❑ False

I have lied about how much money I spent on something I bought.

Partner 1: ❑ True ❑ False   Partner 2: ❑ True ❑ False

I pray every day.

Partner 1: ❑ True ❑ False   Partner 2: ❑ True ❑ False

I love to cuddle.

Partner 1: ❑ True ❑ False   Partner 2: ❑ True ❑ False

I enjoy morning sex.

Partner 1: ❑ True ❑ False   Partner 2: ❑ True ❑ False

I think my partner is a great cook.

Partner 1: ❑ True ❑ False   Partner 2: ❑ True ❑ False

I have talked with a therapist about our relationship.

Partner 1: ❑ True ❑ False   Partner 2: ❑ True ❑ False

I believe our parents make us the way we are.

Partner 1: ❑ True ❑ False   Partner 2: ❑ True ❑ False

I believe that love is always enough.

Partner 1: ❑ True ❑ False   Partner 2: ❑ True ❑ False

RATE MY MATE

This chapter, in which you will give each other a rating from 1 to 10 in various categories, can be a wonderful opportunity to sing unsung praises. Voicing the things you are most grateful for in your partner allows you to show love through appreciation and is something you should remember to do throughout your marriage.

The bottom line is, to have a happy and healthy marriage you must accept each other's flaws, as well as vocalize praise whenever and wherever you can. This chapter can help you identify the small (and big) things you have to offer each other.

For instance, is your spouse patient with children, a reliable friend, or always able to fix the computer? Does your partner nurse you to health when you have a cold, make amazing lasagna, or pay the bills on time every month? Can he or she make you laugh like no one else? Pay attention to each other's unique personality traits and admirable gifts. As one-half of a successful marriage, it is your privilege to receive these gifts, but your job to appreciate them. This chapter will help you identify and sing praise for qualities, talents, and efforts that might have gone unnoticed otherwise.

In addition to completing this chapter, another great exercise can be to create "gratitude lists" for one another. Start by writing down the things you appreciate in each other. Your lists can consist of sweet, funny, even gushy sentiments that express reasons you love each other. You might write things like, "You are a wonderful kisser," "You make the most delicious coffee," "You have sexy legs," or "You bring home pizza when I'm too tired to cook." After you complete your lists, place them in surprising places where the other person will discover them, such as inside a briefcase, nightstand, or refrigerator.

Use the following section to discover, uncover, and remind you of all the special things you appreciate about your partner, as well as the important areas in which you might both improve.

"If I had a flower for every time I thought of you,
I could walk in my garden forever."

– Alfred Lord Tennyson

Rate My Mate

How I'd rate my loved one, on a scale of 1 to 10:
(1 being the lowest, 10 being the highest)

Listening to me:
Partner 1: _____   Partner 2: _____

Telling me he/she loves me:
Partner 1: _____   Partner 2: _____

Anticipating my needs:
Partner 1: _____   Partner 2: _____

Giving advice:
Partner 1: _____   Partner 2: _____

Putting me first:
Partner 1: _____   Partner 2: _____

Expressing himself/herself:
Partner 1: _____   Partner 2: _____

Making me feel sexy:
Partner 1: _____   Partner 2: _____

Making me feel loved:
Partner 1: _____   Partner 2: _____

Spontaneity:
Partner 1: _____   Partner 2: _____

Sex appeal:
Partner 1: _____   Partner 2: _____

Eyes:
Partner 1: _____   Partner 2: _____

Height:
Partner 1: _____   Partner 2: _____

Abs:
Partner 1: _____   Partner 2: _____

Butt:
Partner 1: _____   Partner 2: _____

Kissing:
Partner 1: _____   Partner 2: _____

Foreplay:
Partner 1: _____   Partner 2: _____

Sex:
Partner 1: _____   Partner 2: _____

Cooking:
Partner 1: _____   Partner 2: _____

Laundry:
Partner 1: _____   Partner 2: _____

Washing dishes:

Partner 1: _____   Partner 2: _____

Singing:

Partner 1: _____   Partner 2: _____

Athleticism:

Partner 1: _____   Partner 2: _____

Dancing:

Partner 1: _____   Partner 2: _____

Playing a musical instrument:

Partner 1: _____   Partner 2: _____

Hidden talents:

Partner 1: _____   Partner 2: _____

Being willing to compromise:

Partner 1: _____   Partner 2: _____

Competitive nature:

Partner 1: _____   Partner 2: _____

Personal style:

Partner 1: _____   Partner 2: _____

Hygiene:

Partner 1: _____   Partner 2: _____

Dressing for a special event:

Partner 1: _____   Partner 2: _____

Remembering special occasions:

Partner 1: _____   Partner 2: _____

Picking out gifts:

Partner 1: _____   Partner 2: _____

Massage:

Partner 1: _____   Partner 2: _____

Bad habits:

Partner 1: _____   Partner 2: _____

Being patient:

Partner 1: _____   Partner 2: _____

Fighting fair:

Partner 1: _____   Partner 2: _____

Staying calm during stressful times:

Partner 1: _____   Partner 2: _____

Handling money:

Partner 1: _____   Partner 2: _____

Impulsiveness:

Partner 1: _____   Partner 2: _____

Being driven at work:

Partner 1: _____   Partner 2: _____

Balancing work and time with me:

Partner 1: _____   Partner 2: _____

Balancing time with his/her friends and time with me:

Partner 1: _____   Partner 2: _____

Staying in shape:

Partner 1: _____   Partner 2: _____

Encouraging me to be healthy:

Partner 1: _____   Partner 2: _____

Gossiping:

Partner 1: _____   Partner 2: _____

Being willing to go on an adventure:

Partner 1: _____   Partner 2: _____

Being willing to try new foods:

Partner 1: _____   Partner 2: _____

Being willing to try an extreme sport:

Partner 1: _____   Partner 2: _____

Talking about lovers from the past:

Partner 1: _____   Partner 2: _____

Bringing up old mistakes in a fight:

Partner 1: _____   Partner 2: _____

Snoring:

Partner 1: _____   Partner 2: _____

Procrastinating:

Partner 1: _____   Partner 2: _____

Driving:

Partner 1: _____   Partner 2: _____

Time it takes him/her to get ready to leave the house:

Partner 1: _____   Partner 2: _____

Movie choices:

Partner 1: _____   Partner 2: _____

Planning a date night out for us:

Partner 1: _____   Partner 2: _____

Being romantic:

Partner 1: _____   Partner 2: _____

Writing love notes:

Partner 1: _____   Partner 2: _____

Charming my parents:

Partner 1: _____   Partner 2: _____

THE WEDDING

Although planning your wedding is an exciting and exhilarating time, it can also be a point of contention for many couples. There are many stressors involved in wedding planning, from deciding on a budget to agreeing on the details to hiring and managing vendors. Many times, grooms fail to provide sufficient help with planning. And, of course, we've all heard the horror stories about "Bridezillas." Many couples will eat, sleep, and breathe their wedding up until the big day — no wonder they're so stressed out!

In addition to the nuances of the planning process, wedding planning can bring up personal, emotional, and familial issues. Many couples feel immense pressure to make their wedding day perfect. Some people feel they must have the perfect wedding in order to have the perfect marriage. It is also not uncommon for family members to become overbearing. Unsolicited advice may be an innocent attempt to help, but it can also interfere with and complicate the planning process.

Thus, it is necessary to discuss what you want for your wedding to avoid conflict, anxiety, and meddling family members. Clarify the type of wedding you both want. Does one of you envision a big wedding with hundreds of guests while the other would prefer a small ceremony with just close friends and family? You will also want to decide on a budget that won't break the bank — no one wants to begin their marriage in debt.

Going over your expectations and hopes for your wedding will keep you on-track, on-budget, and as stress-free as you can be. If you make decisions together, you can even have some fun. Going to food tastings and visiting possible venues can be very exciting, if you are communicating throughout the process.

Above all, remember that the true purpose of the wedding is to celebrate your union with the people you care about the most. Enjoy it, and don't let the fun (and even crazy) moments pass you by. Discussing the questions in this chapter can help you avoid much of the stress of planning your wedding.

"If ever two were one, then surely we.
If ever man were loved by wife, then thee."

— Anne Bradstreet

Questions About The Wedding

Do we both want the same kind of wedding (traditional, nontraditional)?

Partner 1: _____

_____

Partner 2: _____

_____

Do we envision our wedding the same way?

Partner 1: _____

_____

Partner 2: _____

_____

Do we want a religious or civil service?

Partner 1: _____

_____

Partner 2: _____

_____

Do we want to get married in a church?

Partner 1: _____

_____

Partner 2: _____

_____

Why did we choose our wedding date?

Partner 1: _____

_____

Partner 2: _____

_____

Why did we choose our wedding location?

Partner 1: _____

_____

Partner 2: _____

_____

Is the wedding-planning process equally important to both of us?

Partner 1: _____

_____

Partner 2: _____

_____

Are the details (stationery, napkins, etc.) equally important to both of us?

Partner 1: _____

_____

Partner 2: _____

_____

Is one of us more involved in the planning than the other?

Partner 1: _____

_____

Partner 2: _____

_____

Do we feel one of us is overly consumed with the wedding?

Partner 1: _____

_____

Partner 2: _____

_____

Have we agreed upon a budget?

Partner 1: _____

_____

Partner 2: _____

_____

Have we agreed upon who pays for what?

Partner 1: _____

_____

Partner 2: _____

_____

How much will our in-laws help in the planning process?

Partner 1: _____

_____

Partner 2: _____

_____

Who will help the most with the planning process?

Partner 1: _____

_____

Partner 2: _____

_____

How will we deal with unsolicited advice from friends and family?

Partner 1: _____

_____

Partner 2: _____

_____

Have we divided planning tasks between us?

Partner 1: _____

_____

Partner 2: _____

_____

How are we feeling about the planning process? Anxious? Excited?

Partner 1: _____

_____

Partner 2: _____

_____

Have we agreed upon the guest list?

Partner 1: _____

_____

Partner 2: _____

_____

Are there people we disagreed about inviting?

Partner 1: _____

_____

Partner 2: _____

_____

What things do we see eye-to-eye on?

Partner 1: _____

_____

Partner 2: _____

_____

What is the toughest decision we will have to make?

Partner 1: _____

_____

Partner 2: _____

_____

What is one thing we disagree about?

Partner 1: _____

_____

Partner 2: _____

_____

How important is it that the woman change her last name after marriage?

Partner 1: _____

_____

Partner 2: _____

_____

What is the funniest thing that has happened during planning?

Partner 1: _____

_____

Partner 2: _____

_____

Describe the most fun part of planning our wedding.

Partner 1: _____

_____

Partner 2: _____

_____

Describe the craziest part of planning the wedding.

Partner 1: _____

_____

Partner 2: _____

_____

Would we rather have our dream wedding or a down payment on a home?

Partner 1: _____

_____

Partner 2: _____

_____

How do we plan to avoid wedding-planning stress?

Partner 1: _____

_____

Partner 2: _____

_____

What are we most looking forward to about the wedding?

Partner 1: _____

_____

Partner 2: _____

_____

Describe our ideal wedding day.

Partner 1: _____

_____

Partner 2: _____

_____

HOPES & DREAMS

American journalist William Allen White once wrote, "I am not afraid of tomorrow, for I have seen yesterday, and I love today." In truth, planning for the future requires you to have patience, be optimistic, and also be realistic about your marriage. When you plan for your future together, imagine that the best is yet to come. Be confident in your dreams. Finally, be flexible with your marriage, and understand that even the best-laid plans can change. Unforeseen roadblocks will appear in your path, so be prepared to deal with the shifts and changes that make up life. Whether you're discussing having children, moving to a new city, buying a home, starting a business, or retirement, be excited about what is next for you as a pair.

Use the questions in this chapter to help you imagine your life in 5, 10, 25, and 50 years. What do you envision? What would be your ideal circumstance? Where might you live? What kinds of material things will you have?

Will you be parents? Homeowners? Career moguls? How you imagine yourselves at different points throughout life is the first step to making goals happen. Furthermore, picturing yourselves together, even after decades, helps strengthen your bond as life partners.

It can also be worthwhile (and fun!) to sit down together and create a list of things you want to do in your lifetime. Some will be simple, such as "try a new cuisine" or "camp out under the stars." Others may call for some planning, such as "plant a garden," "get to know our neighbors," or "build a wine collection." Still other things on your list will require lots of foresight and preparation, such as "visit the Great Wall of China," or "learn to scuba dive." The wonderful part of this exercise is you get to dream together and plan for future adventures. Don't hesitate to add something, no matter how outlandish it seems now — you have your entire lives to complete everything on your list.

Go over the following questions about your hopes, dreams, and visions for your future. Remember, when you dream together, plan for an abundance of happiness, security, and adventure, and do not limit yourselves!

"I am beginning to learn that it is the sweet, simple things of life which are the real ones after all."

– Laura Ingalls Wilder

Questions About Our Hopes & Dreams

What hobby would we like to take up?

Partner 1: _____

_____

Partner 2: _____

_____

What skill would we like to develop?

Partner 1: _____

_____

Partner 2: _____

_____

What is one tradition we would like to keep?

Partner 1: _____

_____

Partner 2: _____

_____

What is one obstacle we have to overcome in our relationship?

Partner 1: _____

_____

Partner 2: _____

_____

Who would we like to spend more time with?

Partner 1: _____

_____

Partner 2: _____

_____

What is one thing we would like to accomplish in the upcoming year?

Partner 1: _____

_____

Partner 2: _____

_____

We think we have lasted this long because:

Partner 1: _____

_____

Partner 2: _____

_____

In the next year, we plan to:

Partner 1: _____

_____

Partner 2: _____

_____

Describe a special trip we plan to take.

Partner 1: _____

_____

Partner 2: _____

_____

We'd like a summer house in:

Partner 1: _____

_____

Partner 2: _____

_____

We'd like a winter house in:

Partner 1: _____

_____

Partner 2: _____

_____

Describe our dream car.

Partner 1: _____

_____

Partner 2: _____

_____

How will we document our past together?

Partner 1: _____

_____

Partner 2: _____

_____

Every day, we are grateful for:

Partner 1: _____

_____

Partner 2: _____

_____

Marriage is a _____ thought for us.

Partner 1: _____

_____

Partner 2: _____

_____

Becoming parents is a _____ thought for us.

Partner 1: _____

_____

Partner 2: _____

_____

How would we like to spend our first anniversary?

Partner 1: _____

_____

Partner 2: _____

_____

How would we like to spend our 10th anniversary?

Partner 1: _____

_____

Partner 2: _____

_____

How would we like to spend our 25th anniversary?

Partner 1: _____

_____

Partner 2: _____

_____

How do we imagine our 50th anniversary?

Partner 1: _____

_____

Partner 2: _____

_____

Where might we want to retire?

Partner 1: _____

_____

Partner 2: _____

_____

Where and how do we picture ourselves in 10 years?

Partner 1: _____

_____

Partner 2: _____

_____

Where and how do we picture ourselves in 25 years?

Partner 1: _____

_____

Partner 2: _____

_____

Where and how do we picture ourselves in 50 years?

Partner 1: _____

_____

Partner 2: _____

_____

What fortune would we like to find in our fortune cookie?

Partner 1: _____

_____

Partner 2: _____

_____

Our final reflections before the wedding:

Partner 1: _____

_____

_____

_____

_____

_____

_____

_____

_____

_____

_____

_____

_____

Partner 2: _____

_____

_____

_____

_____

_____

_____

_____

_____

_____

_____

_____

_____

_____

_____